Watford
in old picture postcards

by Dennis F. Edwards

European Library   ZALTBOMMEL/THE NETHERLANDS

GB ISBN 90 288 1400 0

© 1999 European Library – Zaltbommel/The Netherlands

No part of this book may be reproduced in any form, by print, photoprint, microfilm or any other means, without written permission from the publisher.

Introduction

As we come to the end of the 20th century, many of the famous towns in Britain are being changed not only out of visible recognition, but in their cultural and social make-up as well.

Watford is one of the most prominent examples of how a place has changed in the last forty years due to dynamic and overprogressive local government. The destruction of so much of old Watford some years ago made one elderly resident exclaim: 'I wonder what building is being demolished today.'

Watford has not had a good record of keeping its past or adapting its heritage to modern needs. The destruction of the past began with the demolition of Cassiobury House in 1927. During the period after the Second World War there was an inevitable pause before the needs of very heavy road traffic and flourishing industries, as well as a very popular shopping centre, attracting crowds from all over North London and Hertfordshire, brought about some profound changes. Watford began as a single long street of buildings with insanitary alleyways, rising from the River Colne, to the edge of Cassiobury Park. The Market dates from a Charter granted by King Edward III in 1305. For centuries Watford was dominated by Cassiobury (or Cashiobury as it was once called). Cassiobury was granted by King Henry VIII in 1546 to Sir Richard Morrison, who set about building a house that had 56 rooms and a long gallery. It possibly resembled nearby Chenies Manor. Through marriage, the Morrisons were linked to the Capel family and in the 17th century, Arthur Capel was made the 1st Earl of Essex.

The house was eventually rebuilt, and on 16th April 1680, the diarist John Evelyn came to the house and tells us: 'The house is new, a plaine (sic) fabric built by my friend Mr. Hugh May. There are divers fair and good rooms and excellent carvings by Grinling Gibbons.'

The house was given a large-scale remodelling in the early 19th century by James Wyatt – the style being the romantic Gothic then so fashionable.

A lady visitor, Frances Calvert, in 1816 wrote: 'On Wednesday last we went to Cashiobury, the seat of the Earl of Essex, which is a very pretty house and more full of comforts, curiosities and pretty things than any other house I ever saw.'

The Victorian period was a golden era for Cassiobury, with famous people staying there every weekend. But the ever-mounting costs, and the tide of houses made the estate uneconomic by 1913. Parts of the estate were already being sold for building plots, and the Watford Borough

Council purchased part of the lands for a public park in 1912.

The contents of the great house were sold at a series of auctions from 1922. The vast building did not appeal to the changed tastes of the 1920's and was demolished in 1927, many of the materials going to form new buildings in the town.

Of Watford itself, the arrival of the London and Birmingham Railway in 1837 was soon to have an effect on the local economy. New people arrived to work in the industries that were developing, especially printing. Indeed, by 1939, Watford could justly be called the printing capital of Europe.

The old shops with their small windows and badly-lit interiors gave way to bright new stores, and Watford by 1925 (when the Metropolitan Railway arrived at the edge of the town) became the great shopping centre, not only for Hertfordshire, but also North London.

During the First World War, the Government established large munition factories to the north and south of the town. These areas were later developed into trading estates.

Watford By-pass was constructed between 1924 and 1926, but traffic was to become an ever growing problem. During the years between 1919 and 1939, Watford flourished – new industries, new suburbs. In fact it became two towns – one still provincial – the largest town in Hertfordshire; the other Watford – a suburb for London commuters. Indeed, as Middlesex was built over, the suburbs of Harrow were only 6 miles to the south.

By the early 1960's road traffic had strangled the town and imaginative plans were drawn up and eventually carried out to reduce the problem.

In the 1970's the huge concrete bulk of Charter Place Shopping Centre dominated High Street, to be followed in more recent times by the much better designed (and shopper-friendly) Harlequin Centre. This was officially opened in June 1992. But the effect has been to close most of the old High Street shops. However, there are plans for attractive gardens, cafés and bars – especially towards the famous ponds.

Of course, there are relics of the past, if one knows where to find them. And as this century closes, there is an ever-growing interest in the history we have lost. The 20th century has been a hundred years of profound contrast – nowhere better illustrated than in the town of Watford.

Dennis F. Edwards
Mumbles, Swansea
February 1999

1 The famous gatehouse to Cassiobury Park seen from Rickmansworth Road, a quiet country road in the peaceful days of 1903.

2   Looking out of the Park towards Watford. The gateway was admired by a visitor in 1819: 'An octagonal, tasteful building – ivy clad and honeysuckle and roses cover its top and sides; its back embowered amongst lofty trees.'

3   More than fifty years have passed since the previous view of the gateway. The structure was demolished in 1971 for the Rickmansworth Road widening scheme.

4 The west front of Cassiobury 1906, showing the Gothic style architecture in which James Wyatt covered the 17th century house. The famous painter J. M. Turner produced scenes of the house during 1804 and 1805.

5 Cassiobury as it was in the days when Adèle, Countess of Essex, entertained Edwardian society here – including the King.

6   Cassiobury Park was also used for public events at certain times. This event took place in July 1855, when the Watford Horticultural and Floricultural Show took place. The 'Illustrated London News' reported: '… although Londoners lately witnessed … grand floricultural displays at the Crystal Palace at Sydenham, the park of which is, however, a much less delightful place for a flower show than the beautiful domain of Cassiobury.'

The show was open from 2 till 5 o'clock, and many local shops closed so that Watford people could attend.

7   The Swiss Cottage by the River Gade, Rickmansworth Road. It was one of a number of ornate buildings designed by Jeffrey Wyatville for the Earl of Essex in the early years of the 19th century. This cottage had stained glass windows depicting the customs and costumes of Switzerland. It is now the only surviving lodge.

SWISS COTTAGE, CASSIOBURY, WATFORD.

8 The old water mill on the Gade (demolished 1966). Originally a corn mill, it later served to pump water from the river to the mansion.

9 Cassiobury Lock on the Grand Union Canal – a place little changed over the years. The canal opened as far as Kings Langley in 1797; the engineer was William Jessop. Both the Earl of Essex and the Earl of Clarendon (at nearby The Grove) tolerated the canal because they felt it would little disturb their rural seclusion, but the Canal Company had to pay £15,000 and £500 compensation respectively.

10 The Grove, seat of the Villiers family (the Clarendon title created in 1776). The house mainly dates from 1756, with major alterations in 1788 and 1850. The estate was sold to the London, Midland and Scottish Railway in 1939. It is now a business college.

11 A rare photograph from June 1915, showing men of the 1st and 4th Norfolk Regiment practising 'hop pole' bridge building on the river Gade.

12 Now the war is over! Peace procession July 1919 through the public area of Cassiobury (acquired by the Council in 1912).

13 It hardly seems possible that today this is one of the busiest parts of Watford. But the junction of the Rickmansworth, Hempstead, St. Albans and High Street roads looked like this ninety years ago. To celebrate the Jubilee of Queen Victoria in 1887, 'a fine young oak from Cassiobury' was planted at the crossroads by the Countess of Essex, with the Earl of Essex and town dignitaries and the band of the Watford Volunteers in attendance.

14   By 1936 traffic problems at the crossroads saw the oak chopped down and a traffic roundabout installed. The house in the trees on the left is The Elms, shortly to be demolished for the new Town Hall.

15 The roundabout and the new Town Hall about 1948. The building was designed in plain and functional style by C. Cowles Vosey (son of the famous Charles Vosey) and the foundation stone was laid in May 1938.

16 The Town Hall was only just completed in September 1939 as the Second World War began and was not fully used by the Council until 1946.

17 Watford's famous pond is the only surviving example of a number of pools that were a natural feature in ancient times and used by cattle and horses. The estate on the far right belonged to John Sedgewick, solicitor and clerk to the Watford Local Board (council).

18 The pond about 1903. There was a ramp so that horses and carts could enter the water for both cleaning and drinking. To the left is Northend House, with the crossroads and The Elms in the far distance.

19 The old houses and their wooded grounds have been replaced by shops and the pond has been landscaped. To the top right a Green Line coach is just passing the roundabout, whilst on the left are the 'Tudorbethan' style premises of Cakebread and Robey, for many years a well-known builders' merchant store. The company also had showrooms at Station Road in Harrow. The building is now a café bar.

20 Back to the early days and a horse and cart cool down in the pond one hot afternoon about 1904. Darby's Nursery on the right had extensive grounds stretching back to Weymouth Street.

21 The same place some fifty years later, with parades of shops built in the late 1930's on the site of John Sedgewick's house.

22   The view looking the other way towards the town centre. Note the Plaza Café on the left, seen here next to the Odeon Cinema. The original cinema opened here in April 1929 as The Plaza, but was taken over by the Odeon Circuit in October 1936 and re-named. Later the building was demolished and the second Odeon was a re-naming of the old Gaumont Cinema in 1964.

23 The pond area about 1961. Monmouth House was originally built in 1610 by Sir Robert Carey, Duke of Monmouth, and it eventually became the Dower house for the Essex family. Altered many times – including being converted into separate houses – it was skilfully transformed into modern shops and commercial premises in 1927, using materials salvaged from Cassiobury House.

24 Across the road stood the Old Fire Station and Upton House (used as Council Offices until 1939). The whole block of buildings here was swept away in one of the first great 'improvements' in the 1960's, being replaced by Gade House (opened on 28 January 1965).

25 It's sale time at Clements in 1907. On the extreme right is Sainsburys, with one of their horse-drawn delivery carts outside. Alfred Clement opened his drapery 'emporium' here in 1898.

26 Clement's store began to expand in the 1900's and Mr. Clement announced that 'Our assistants have strict instructions not to press any article on an unwilling customer'. Clements are still trading from the same site today.

27 The year is 1960 and the view is of High Street looking towards Monmouth House, with Upton House on the left. Many of the once famous High Street shops have long disappeared.

28 There seems to be no traffic problem in Market Place near the junction with Clarendon Road in 1912. The lime trees grew in front of the Lime Tree Temperance Hotel. The buildings here were later called Dudley's Corner. Across the street the tall building, next to the white fronted Empress Tea Rooms, is Bucks, a well-known and long established bakery and caterer.

29   Market Place with the Essex Arms and the Corn Exchange, and Longleys drapery store. The Tuesday market can be seen on the left.

30 An interesting selection of road vehicles, old and new, in this study of Market Place just after the First World War. Just behind the man on the horse cart are The Empress Tea Rooms and restaurant, opened on the site of Derry House on 25th July 1916. Note the lime trees on the right.

31 A step back into time – and this is what Market Place looked like at the end of stagecoaching days, just before the railway came in 1837. The Essex Arms is on the left, and in the distance is the old Market Hall near the church. The hall was destroyed by fire in 1853.

32 Market Place 1927. The Empress Tea Rooms (right) were possibly intended as the site for the terminus of the Metropolitan Railway branch from Moor Park. But the original plans were greatly modified because of objections to the proposed railway having to cross Cassiobury Park. When the line opened in 1925, the station was inconveniently terminated at the edge of Cassiobury, a mile from the town centre.

33 Market Day at Watford 1905. The Essex Arms (left) was an important centre for social life for centuries. In the days when it was owned by Trust Houses, lunch cost 30p and afternoon tea 15p. The hotel closed down in 1929.

34 Market Place at the beginning of the 20th century. The tall building on the left was the Bucks and Oxon Bank (later Lloyds). On the right of the picture the white building is The Compasses, dating from 1726 or earlier. Later the pub was rebuilt and medieval remains were found in the wall, a fragment of which is now preserved at the corner of Market Street. Beyond can be seen The Rose and Crown, the other principal inn of the town.

35 Cattle were still sold in the middle of the street at Market Place until 1927. For years there were complaints – 'Anyone can go with a flock of sheep … sell them … the stench they leave is indescribable' complained a councillor. The Rose and Crown on the right was built on part of a large area of land owned by Merton College, Oxford. Eventually the land was sold and Market Street laid out. Merton road commemorates the original owners, and the Roman Catholic church was also built on the same land.

36 Market Place at Christmas 1934. Cawdells rebuilt department store occupied the site of the Essex Arms and the Corn Exchange. The business was founded by James Cawdell (died 1941) who took over the drapery shop of Longleys in 1905. Part of the site was occupied by Timothy Whites and Taylors, the household store, who opened here in May 1931.

37 View taken one morning in about 1948. An STL-type bus on route 142 – West Kilburn to Watford Junction – stops outside The Rose and Crown. Cawdells were offering oak bedroom suites for £9-90p.

38 Market Place 1960, with a London Transport country bus (route 346 to Kingswood) on the left. Across the street, a Scammel (Watford-built) 'mechanical horse' owned by British Railways is delivering goods.

39 A view further down High Street back in 1906 near the premises of Frederick Downer, whose well-equipped photographic studios were patronised 'by a number of noble and aristocratic patrons'. It was Downer's local views, and also those of Coles of Queen's Road, that were used for many postcards. Infortunately, many of their glass negatives were lost in the 1960's during the wide-spread clearance of central Watford.

40 St. Mary's Church dates back to Norman days, although the tower is 15th century. There was a restoration in 1848 and a major one in 1871, when the exterior walls were clad in flints. The fine east window was destroyed in an air raid during the Second World War.

41 St. Mary's, with the old church schools on the left. They were founded in 1841 and were here until 1922. In the distance can be seen Ballards Buildings and the One Bell public house.

42 The Old Vicarage stood on the south side of the churchyard from 1630 until 1916.

43 As Watford grew, so did the need for more churches. St. Andrew's, Park Road, was designed in 1857 by Sebastian Sanders Teulon. The church was attended by many of the railway workers living in this new part of Victorian Watford.

44 The interior of St. Michael and All Angels at the junction of Mildred Avenue and Durban Road. The foundation stone was laid on 30th September 1911 and the church was consecrated in 1913. The building of the church owned much to the funds raised by Mildred Schreiber, who lived at Dulton House in Lower High Street).

45 A return to the town centre and a busy scene in High Street near the junction with Queen's Road (left) and King Street. The building with the dome was for many years the premises of Boots, and in more recent times Ketts electrical retailers. It now stands at the entrance to the Harlequin Centre. Also on the left is the Eight Bells, which is recorded in 1753 as The Barley Mow.

46 High Street, with Barclays Bank left on the corner of King Street. The bank buildings date from 1911. King Street was laid out by Jonathan King of Watford Place in 1851, when he converted what had been the drive to the house.

47 Looking up hill from Lower High Street about 1965. Many of the rather untidy shop fronts mask much earlier structures. During restoration work at this time at number 137, a mural depicting the Royal Arms of James I was discovered (now in Watford Museum).

48 By the 1880's, Watford was expanding and the area around St. Albans Road was built up. Small industries established and a separate suburb developed. The Watford Electric Coliseum cinema opened along here in 1918.

49 Salesman's card advertising the clothing establishment of J. R. Gale at 158 St. Alban's Road about 1902. There seems very little space left in the windows! Mr. Gale stocked not only garments for men and women, but curtains and floor coverings as well.

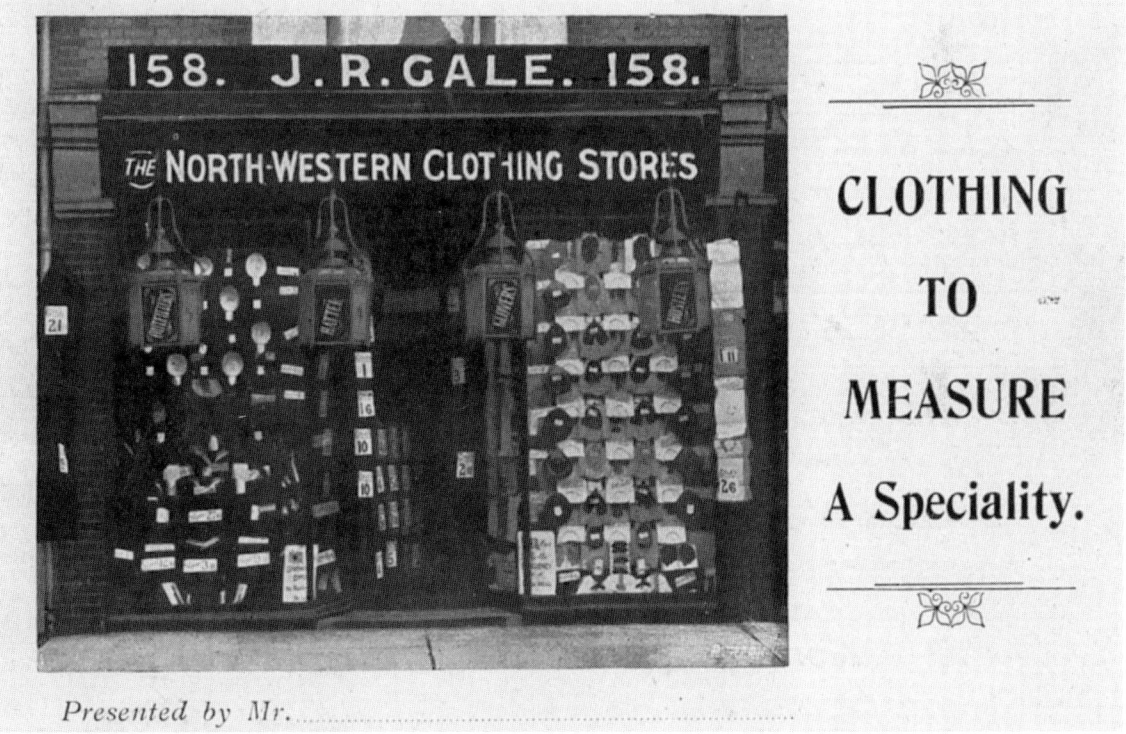

50 Clarendon Road was the grandest of the new roads – laid out from the old High Street. Named after the Earl of Clarendon of The Grove, it was opened in 1864. It was lined with large and sometimes ugly mansions owned by local businessmen and the more affluent 'commuters' who worked in London. The tower and spire of the Congregational church on the left. Now all has been transformed into a street of office blocks and private car parks.

51 Vicarage Road is now not only a well-known Watford street, but a name known throughout the football world. The famous football ground at the far end was opened on 30th August 1922. The gates on the left mark the entrance to the cemetery, opened in 1858.

52 Extraordinary scene at Vicarage Road by the cemetery gates on Tuesday, 3rd October 1905. Vast crowds of mourners and just curious Watford people have turned out for the funeral of Mary Money, a local girl who had worked as a bar maid in Lavender Hill, London. Her body was found in the Merstham Tunnel on the London Brighton and South Coast Railway, south of Croydon on 24th September – and foul play was suspected.

53 Queen's Road by the junction with High Street. Laid out in 1860, the road was at one time called Queen Street. The section seen here is now entirely obliterated except as a pedestrian entrance to the Harlequin Centre.

54 On the right in this rather gloomy view of Queen's Road is the Watford School of Science and Art, and the Public Library. The buildings were opened in 1874 under the patronage of the Earl of Clarendon. Later, in more recent times, Sainsbury had a branch along this part of the road. The school buildings were destroyed by fire about twenty years ago.

55 Queen's Road looking toward the town centre from Derby Road. The Methodist Church and the Post Office are on the right. The Post Office opened here in 1885. Beyond are the premises of Trewin Brothers. All has now been swept away by the pedestrianisation of the area and the building of new roads and pedestrian underpasses.

56 Watford's third large department store was Trewin Brothers further along Queen's Road, near the junction with Derby Road. F. T. Trewin purchased an existing shop and converted it into a general department store. In 1926 the store advertised: 'The shopping centre where everything for the house and wardrobe can be obtained.' The business was later acquired by the John Lewis Partnership and after the Second World War, a new building was erected. The new and much larger Trewins opened in the Harlequin Centre on 19th August 1990.

57 The Empire Picture Hall, Merton Road, opened its doors for entertainment on 6th November 1913 and has been in business ever since. Equipment for showing sound films was installed in August 1929,

58 The London Orphan Asylum was founded in Clapham in 1815 and moved out to the more salubrious air of Hertfordshire, just north of Watford Station, in 1871.

London Orphan Asylum Front, Watford.

59 The range of buildings was designed by Henry Dawson in an institutional and gloomy style. The opening ceremony was performed by Princess Mary, Duchess of Tec. The institution was later known as Reeds School.

60 A fine aerial view of Watford in the 1960's. Watford Grammar School for Girls (dating from 1907) is in the foreground. At the top right of the picture Watford Place and one of the early modern office blocks can be seen.

61 Floods in the lower part of the town have been a hazard for centuries. This view dates from 22nd July 1907. The bus is on the Callowlands, Watford Junction-Bushey service. A reporter in 1878 witnessed a flood and was greatly amused to see local residents carrying their pigs and chickens up to the bedrooms to save them from drowning.

62 A fine early illustration of a train crossing the arches over the river Colne in 1840. The architect for the London and Birmingham Railway was John Rennie. Because of the soft composition of the ground, the arches were laid on brushwood foundations.

63 Because of strong objections from both Essex and Clarendon, the new railway was routed to the north of Watford and a tunnel had to be built so that neither landowner could see or hear the trains. Building the Watford tunnel cost eleven lives and many workers were injured.

WATFORD TUNNEL FACE, JUNE 6TH 1837.

64 John Rennie's classical portal can be seen, as one of the first trains on the new railway enters the tunnel 'wrong line' because of the unfinished work. The London and Birmingham Railway was the world's first long distance main line. The first section was opened from Euston as far as Boxmoor in 1837.

65 The first Watford station was sited west of the St. Alban's Road. But after the building of the branch line to St. Alban's in May 1858, the station was built on its present site. The Clarendon Hotel (left) was opened to serve a new class of client – the commercial business traveller.

66 As time passed traffic grew on the line and a second tunnel had to be built and the line quadrupled from London. The branch to Rickmansworth via High Street opened and there was a growing commuter traffic. This view of the junction station dates from about 1912.

67 After the Second World War – a scene on a quiet Sunday about 1946. Next to the Dublin poster on the far right is a London Transport sign directing passengers to the Bakerloo Line terminus. Bakerloo trains reached Watford as early as 1917, part of a grand scheme of electrified lines from London, although electric trains ran from Euston and Broad Street in 1922.

68 North-bound express and local trains at Bushey water troughs south of Watford a century ago. The Watford suburban tracks were later constructed on the right hand side of the railway.

69 A London and North Western Railway 'Scotch' express at Bushey troughs ninety years ago.

70 At the same spot in 1939, with an LMS north-bound express for Glasgow headed by Number 6203 'Princess Margaret Rose'.

71 One of a series of advertisements issued by the London and North Western Railway just before 1914. Euston electric trains did not begin until 1922, but Bakerloo Line tube trains ran over the new tracks during the First World War, possibly to bring thousands of workers to the Government munition factories just north of Watford Junction.

LIVE IN THE COUNTRY.

The Opening of the New L. & N.W. Line between Willesden and Watford on February 10th with

new stations at Harlesden, Stonebridge Park, North Wembley, Kenton, Headstone Lane, Watford West, and Croxley Green, has opened up an entirely new Residential District to the City Man.

This District has been very appropriately called

LONDON'S BEAUTIFUL NORTH-WEST

and, commencing February 10th, the train service from and to Euston will be considerably augmented, making it especially convenient to the City Man.

Cheap Rents.   **Perfect Sanitation.**   **Good Schools.**
Excellent Golf Courses.   **Ample Water Supply.**

Send a post card to Enquiry Office, Euston Station, N.W., for free booklet entitled "North-Western Country Homes."

North-Western Country Homes.

72 After 1919 regular motor bus services were resumed at Watford and a number of operators began routes. This is a London General Country bus about 1931.

73 The National Bus Company was founded by Thomas Clarkson and covered a wide area of the countryside to the north of London. Here a bus on route 306 waits at the terminus.

74 The Metropolitan Railway and the London and North Eastern Railway built the new branch line from Moor Park, and also from Rickmansworth, to the edge of Watford in 1925. This is the opening ceremony on Watford Metropolitan Station 31st October 1925. The Mayor of Watford, Alderman M. A. Thorpe, and the Town Clerk, with Lord Faringdon, Chairman of the LNER (left), and Lord Aberconway (Chairman of the Metropolitan) on the right.

75 Watford Met station has never been busy. Here a 'T' stock train waits in vain for passengers one day in the late 1940's. Part of the seldom-used cattle dock and freight yard is to the right.

76 The last picture is of transport of a different kind! A horse-drawn cart selling vegetables to some jolly Asian ladies, Durban Road 1994. A last link between the old style of Watford life and the new.